Every Kid's Guide to
Handling Fights with
Brothers or Sisters

Written by
JOY BERRY

CHILDRENS PRESS ®
CHICAGO

About the Author and Publisher

Joy Berry's mission in life is to help families cope with everyday problems and to help children become competent, responsible, happy individuals. To achieve her goal, she has written over two hundred self-help books for children from birth through age twelve. Her work revolutionized children's publishing by providing families with practical, how-to, living skills information that was previously unavailable in children's books.

Joy gathered a dedicated team of experts, including psychologists, educators, child developmentalists, writers, editors, designers, and artists, to form her publishing company and to help produce her work.

The company, Living Skills Press, produces thoroughly researched books and audio-visual materials that successfully combine humor and education to teach subjects ranging from how to clean a bedroom to how to resolve problems and get along with other people.

Managing Editor: Ellen Klarberg
Copy Editor: Kate Dickey
Contributing Editors: Libby Byers, Nancy Cochran, Maureen Dryden,
Yona Flemming, Kathleen Mohr, Susan Motycka
Editorial Assistant: Sandy Passarino

Art Director: Laurie Westdahl
Design: Abigail Johnston, Laurie Westdahl
Production: Abigail Johnston, Caroline Rennard
Illustrations designed by: Bartholomew
Inker: Caroline Rennard
Colorer: Tuan Pham
Composition: Curt Chelin

If you are like most children, you probably fight with your brothers or sisters.

In **EVERY KID'S GUIDE TO HANDLING FIGHTS WITH BROTHERS OR SISTERS** you will learn the following:

- ten reasons why brothers and sisters fight,
- why fighting is harmful, and
- four steps for avoiding fights with your brothers or sisters.

There are many reasons why you fight with your brothers or sisters.

Reason 1. Wanting your parents' love

If you are like most children, you probably love your parents more than anyone else. Because your parents are so important to you, you probably wish they would love you more than anyone else.

Sometimes you might feel that your parents love your brothers or sisters more than they love you. This might upset you.

It might make you feel angry with your brothers or sisters and make you want to fight with them.

Do not fight if you feel that your parents love your brothers or sisters more than they love you. Do these things instead:

Remember this: Although most parents love their children equally, they usually love each child in a special way. They know each child is not like anyone else and cannot be replaced by anyone else.

Because you are one of a kind, your parents love you in a way that is special from the way they love your brothers or sisters.

Talk to your parents. Ask them to tell you about the things that make you special to them.

Think about these things if you feel your parents love your brothers or sisters more than they love you.

Reason 2. Wanting to be the best

If you are like most children, you probably wish you were better than anyone else in the way you
- think,
- look, and
- act.

In some ways, your brothers or sisters might be smarter than you. You might think they are better looking. They might be able to do something better than you. This might upset you.

You might feel jealous and want to fight with your brothers or sisters.

Do not fight when you are jealous of your brothers' or sisters' special qualities or skills. Do these things instead:

Remember this: No one person can be the best at everything. Every person has both strengths and weaknesses. Your brothers or sisters might be better than you in some ways. But most likely you are better than them in other ways.

Talk to your family and friends. Ask them to tell you about the things you do well.

Think about these things whenever you feel that your brothers or sisters are better than you.

Reason 3. Wanting to be respected

If you are like most people, you want people to respect your

- body,
- feelings, and
- thoughts.

Sometimes your brothers or sisters might treat you disrespectfully. They might hurt you or your feelings. They might do things that make you feel bad about the way you think. This might upset you.

You might get angry and want to fight with your brothers or sisters.

Do not fight when your brothers or sisters treat you disrespectfully. Do these things instead:

Remember this: Most people will not be disrespectful to people who treat them with respect. If you treat your brothers or sisters respectfully, they will most likely treat you the same way.

Talk to your brothers or sisters when they are disrespectful. Tell them how you feel. Ask them to stop.

Talk to your parents. If your brothers or sisters continue to act disrespectfully, ask your parents to help you deal with them.

Reason 4. Wanting to be treated fairly

If you are like most people, you want to be treated fairly. You want to receive your fair share of

- things,
- attention, and
- privileges.

You also do not want to do more than your fair share of work.

Sometimes your brothers or sisters might get more of something than you do. Sometimes they might not have to work as hard as you do. This might upset you.

You might feel cheated and want to fight with your brothers or sisters.

Do not fight when you feel that you are being treated unfairly. Do these things instead:

Remember this: Things between people do not always have to be equal in order to be fair. Sometimes your brothers or sisters might get more than you. Other times you might get more than they do. Things usually even out in the end.

Ask questions if you feel things are not fair between you and your brothers or sisters. Sometimes your questions might help other people see that you are not being treated fairly. They might realize that something should be done to correct the problem.

Other times your questions might help you understand the situation better. You might realize that you *are* being treated fairly.

Reason 5. Not wanting to be teased

When people tease you, they make fun of you in playful ways. If you are like most people, there are times when you do not want to be teased.

Sometimes your brothers or sisters might tease you when you do not want to be teased. This might upset you.

You might become annoyed and want to fight with your brothers or sisters.

Do not fight with your brothers or sisters when they tease you. Do these things instead:

Remember this: People who tease often enjoy annoying and upsetting others. Becoming annoyed or upset only encourages these people to continue teasing you. To discourage them, you should try to stay calm whenever you are being teased.

Ignore your brothers or sisters when they tease you.

Walk away from them if you find that it is too difficult for you to ignore them. Your brothers or sisters cannot tease you if you are not around them.

Reason 6. Not wanting to be embarrassed

When people embarrass you, they put you down or humiliate you.

Being embarrassed can cause you to feel bad about yourself. If you are like most people, you do not want other people to embarrass you.

Sometimes your brothers or sisters might say or do something to embarrass you. This might upset you.

You might feel hurt and want to fight with your brothers or sisters.

Do not fight when your brothers or sisters embarrass you. Do these things instead:

Remember this: No one, including your brothers or sisters, likes to be embarrassed. Your brothers or sisters do not want you to embarrass them any more than you want them to embarrass you.

Make an agreement with your brothers or sisters. Promise that you will not embarrass them if they will not embarrass you.

Walk away if your brothers or sisters forget their promise and embarrass you. They can't embarrass you if you are not there to embarrass.

Reason 7. Not wanting your belongings abused

If you are like most people, you do not want other people to use your belongings without asking your permission. You also do not want your belongings to be

- lost,
- misused,
- damaged, or
- destroyed.

Sometimes your brothers or sisters might use your belongings without your permission. Sometimes they might abuse your belongings. This might upset you.

You might become angry and want to fight with your brothers or sisters.

Do not fight when your brothers or sisters abuse your belongings. Do these things instead:

Remember this: You own your belongings. As long as you do not hurt yourself or anyone else, you can do whatever you want with them. This means that you can share them or insist that no one else use them.

Talk to your brothers or sisters if they abuse your things. Together you can decide what needs to be done to make things better.

Talk to your parents. If your brothers or sisters won't cooperate with you, ask your parents to work things out.

You can keep your brothers or sisters from abusing your belongings if you

- do not lend your belongings to your brothers or sisters if you think they might abuse them;
- put your belongings away so your brothers or sisters cannot use them without your permission.

Reason 8. Wanting privacy

Privacy is time you spend by yourself. If you are like most people, you need a certain amount of privacy.

Sometimes you want to be alone to think and daydream. You might want to be by yourself to do something without being distracted or disturbed.

Sometimes your brothers or sisters might disturb your privacy. They might insist on bothering you or being with you when you want to be alone. This might upset you.

You might become irritated and want to fight with your brothers or sisters.

Do not fight when your brothers or sisters disturb your privacy. Do these things instead:

Remember this: Everyone, including your brothers or sisters, has the right to have privacy. If you respect your brothers' or sisters' right to have privacy, they will most likely respect your right to have privacy.

Talk to your brothers or sisters when you want privacy. Tell them you want to be alone.

Go to a safe place where you can be alone.

Tell someone where you are going so no one will think you are lost or will worry about you.

Reason 9. Being together too much

Most brothers and sisters live together. They spend a lot of time and do a lot of things with each other. Sometimes people who are together a lot get tired of each other.

Sometimes you might get tired of being with your brothers or sisters. This might upset you.

You might become irritated and want to fight with your brothers or sisters.

Do not fight with your brothers or sisters when you are tired of being around them. Do these things instead:

Remember this: It is normal for people to get tired of each other when they are together too much. Your brothers or sisters probably get tired of being around you just as much as you get tired of being around them.

Tell your brothers or sisters when you feel you are spending too much time together.

Get away from them if you feel you are getting tired of each other.

Reason 10. Feeling safe

If you are like most people, you might fight with your brothers or sisters because you feel it is safe to fight with them.

Friends can stop being friends, but brothers or sisters cannot stop being brothers or sisters.

A fight might end a friendship, but it cannot end a relationship between brothers or sisters.

When you are angry or upset, you might fight with your brothers or sisters since you feel there is no danger of losing them.

Unfortunately, bad things can happen when you fight with your brothers or sisters.

You can hurt each other
- physically or
- emotionally.

You can also damage or destroy each other's belongings. Therefore, you should avoid fighting with your brothers or sisters.

Do not start a fight with your brothers or sisters. If they start a fight with you, follow these four steps:

Step 1. Think about it.

Do you want to get hurt?

Do you really want to hurt your brother or sister?

Step 2. Talk about it.

When your brothers or sisters want to start a fight, stand face to face and look into their eyes. Ask them why they want to fight. Ask them not to fight with you.

If talking doesn't help, try this:

Step 3. Walk or run away.

If your brothers or sisters come after you, try this:

Step 4. Go get help.

Ask an older person such as a parent or baby sitter
to help you deal with your brothers or sisters.

If you are like most people, there might be times when you wish you didn't have brothers or sisters. But before you wish too hard,

Remember this: Sometimes life can be pretty boring and awfully lonely without brothers or sisters.